Foreword／はじめに

For the past decade, I have been trying to develop improved forms of TOEIC® L&R instruction that will better benefit students and help them achieve higher scores on the TOEIC® L&R Test. With reading, the answer for improving your score is simple: you must practice, practice, practice. The reading questions in this book were written with a specific level an[...] [...]tion (travel, hotels, office) in mind. This is to help students anticipate the c[...] [...]aimed at their English level. This should lead to succ[...] [...]nts to practice further. Doing this is the only way o[...] [...]OEIC® L&R reading ability.

Matthew Wilson

. . . .

TOEIC® L&R リーディングスコアアップのためには、基礎的な文法力と語彙力、そして TOEIC® L&R の形式を知り慣れることが大切です。本書はそれらの能力を総合的に高めることを目的に編集されていますので、この一冊を繰り返しやるだけでも TOEIC® L&R に求められる文法力と語彙力、そして頻出問題のシーンやパターンを知ることが可能です。問題に取り組むむときは、書かれている状況を推測しながら読み進めましょう。パート５とパート６の文法、語彙問題は繰り返し問題を解いてください。パート６の文章挿入問題とパート７は、本文の中に必ず答えを見つけるための手がかりがあるはずです。解法のためのプロセスが本書を通して見えてくるはずです。

鶴岡　公幸

. . . .

英語はスポーツと同じです。サッカーで勝つために、基本のドリブル練習や、実践での練習試合を重ねるのと同様に、TOEIC® L&R のリーディングスコアアップにも、「語彙力」と「文法力」の基本のルールを覚え、実際に「解く」実践トレーニングが必須です。本書では、最新の『頻出語彙問題』、『頻出文法問題』で基礎を固めながら、『出題パターンに慣れる』実践練習が可能です。また、TOEIC® L&R のリーディングセクションでは、限りある制限時間を上手に配分し、得意なテーマの問題でより得点を獲ることが鍵となります。本書は、頻出テーマに分かれているため、自分が得意なテーマ、苦手なテーマを知ることができます。学習は、自分の弱点を知ることから始まります。学習後には、復習するべき項目が明確になるはずです。本書が、多くの方の TOEIC® L&R スコアアップ、英語力向上に役立つことを願っています。

佐藤　千春

Business World

Incomplete Sentences

Select the best answer to complete the sentence. Then choose the letter (A), (B), (C), or (D).

1. The ------- technology used for coffee mugs by ABC Outdoors keeps surfaces from getting too hot.

   (A) warm   (B) frequent   (C) unattached   (D) innovative

2. Our business depends on providing high quality printing quickly and -------.

   (A) affordably   (B) affordable   (C) afford   (D) affordability

3. This special offer is available ------- to customers on our mailing list.

   (A) exclusively   (B) financially   (C) relatively   (D) productively

4. Insurance should ------- your factory for any earthquake and typhoon damage.

   (A) dismantle   (B) compensate   (C) retain   (D) improve

5. ------- it is unspoken, we tend to choose applicants based upon their perceived emotional intelligence.

   (A) Anyway   (B) Through   (C) Yet   (D) Although

6. Ringo Computers had an increase in revenue due to a good year-end sales -------.

   (A) performed   (B) performing   (C) performance   (D) performer

7. The next major software update ------- to be released in March sometime.

   (A) expected   (B) expecting   (C) is expecting   (D) is expected

8. The clearance sale on winter wear will serve to reduce ------- of older products.

   (A) clothes   (B) interest   (C) inventory   (D) devices

Text Completion

Select the best answer to complete the text. Then choose the letter (A), (B), (C), or (D).

Question 9-12 refer to the following advertisement.

When you run a small business, your time is extremely valuable. MyCounter is an office app that tracks where ------ second of your computer time is going,
9.
making it ideal for anyone who needs to record time spent on clients. Track as many projects or clients as you ------, view colorful graphs, export timesheets,
10.
and sync your numbers with several project management apps. ------, your
11.
employees can use MyCounter, and you can divide them into different groups to stay organized. MyCounter is free for up to five users. ------. This version
12.
has other features to help the small business owner stay on top of things, all for this a very low price.

9. (A) all   (B) almost   (C) every   (D) total

10. (A) want   (B) wanted   (C) wanting   (D) have wanted

11. (A) Best of all   (B) All things considered   (C) Therefore   (D) It goes without saying

12. (A) Interested persons should contact their nearest small business.
     (B) Businesses of more than 5 employees are considered mid-sized.
     (C) MyCounter will find you the right employee for the job.
     (D) MyCounter Pro allows unlimited users for $5 per user, per month.

Part 7

Reading Comprehension

Question 13-15 refer to the following advertisement.

Everyone has the right to drink pure, clean water, especially at home. To ensure that you and your family have healthy drinking water, a water purification system is indispensable.

Cleanwater Inc. has a line of home water filters designed to protect you from harmful industrial and agricultural environmental pollutants in tap water. We carry countertop or under-counter systems, each manufactured with state-of-the-art filters. All you have to do is change the filter every 12,000 gallons (about every six months).

We give customers a price guarantee as well as a 30-day money back guarantee. We offer free shipping on all orders of $50.00 or more. If you have any questions or feedback, please call us toll free at 1-900-G19-FREE. All major credit cards, money orders and checks are accepted.

---

13. According to the advertisement, what is one source of water pollution?
    (A) Agricultural waste
    (B) Domestic waste
    (C) Microorganisms
    (D) Oil spills

14. How often should the filters be replaced?
    (A) Twice a year
    (B) Every month
    (C) Every three months
    (D) When the filter turns color

15. When does the customer NOT pay for delivery?
    (A) Whenever buying their products
    (B) When products are returned
    (C) When the filter breaks down
    (D) When purchases are over 50 dollars

Express trains to be suspended over global health crisis

New York – NYC Railway Co. said Friday it will reduce services on its express train line between NYC and WDC stations later this month, due to a plunge in passengers amid the outbreak of the new virus.

The company will cancel some of the express trains on the line from next Thursday to March 31, with the number of trains to be suspended reaching up to 17 per day. A total of 92 express trains will be canceled during the period.

Many of the trains to be suspended are those planned to meet an expected surge in travel demand during the spring break period. The company will allow people who have purchased tickets for the affected express trains to switch to other trains or get a refund.

All other trains between NYC and WDC will be operated as scheduled during the period, the company said.

On Tuesday, the official of the train company said that the number of passengers in the first nine days of March decreased 56 percent from a year before, apparently reflecting growing moves among companies and people to avoid business and sightseeing trips amid the health crisis.

16. What is the reason that the train company will reduce services?

(A) To avoid traffic congestion
(B) To respond to a lack of demand
(C) To keep passengers safe
(D) To promote alternate services

17. What is NOT mentioned in this article?

(A) Passengers who have bought tickets will get a refund.
(B) The number of passengers in early March decreased from the previous year.
(C) Passengers will not be able to change their tickets without paying an extra fee.
(D) All trains, except for express trains, will operate as usual.

Scene 2

Education

Part 5

Incomplete Sentences

Select the best answer to complete the sentence. Then choose the letter (A), (B), (C), or (D).

1. Mr. Hashimoto ------- in business administration.

   (A) consists   (B) interests   (C) inspects   (D) specializes

2. Our school has a ------- curriculum across all departments.

   (A) comprehensions   (B) comprehend   (C) comprehensive   (D) comprehension

3. Application forms for scholarships are distributed at information sessions ------- early to mid-April.

   (A) in   (B) among   (C) against   (D) on

4. Students are encouraged to challenge ------- through research and study on a daily basis.

   (A) themselves   (B) theirs   (C) their   (D) they

5. Students can explore areas of ------- interest and develop their own learning styles.

   (A) tentative   (B) potential   (C) knowledgeable   (D) particular

6. Course content and delivery are tailored to the needs and ------- of individual students.

   (A) expects   (B) expectations   (C) expecting   (D) expectant

7. The ------- for the next semester will be withdrawn from your bank account on Wednesday.

   (A) fund   (B) price   (C) tuition   (D) charge

8. Applications for dormitories are accepted six months ------- the expected starting date of your stay.

   (A) in order to   (B) prior to   (C) except for   (D) on top of

Text Completion

Select the best answer to complete the text. Then choose the letter (A), (B), (C), or (D).

Questions 9-12 refer to the following web page.

> The University of Detroit offers awards to undergraduate students to recognize outstanding achievement at different levels of study. ------, the university
> **9.**
> awards approximately 4,500 admission scholarships totaling nearly $20 million. Plus, students have access to nearly 5,900 in-course scholarships during the school year. ------. Students are permitted to combine awards so keep
> **10.**
> applying for awards ------ you are admitted to the university. For more general
> **11.**
> information on ------, please visit the University of Detroit Awards page.
> **12.**

9. (A) Total   (B) In sum   (C) To recap   (D) Overall

10. (A) These scholarships are for current students who are excelling in their programs.
    (B) Our university is difficult to be accepted to, so good luck with your application.
    (C) To find out more about your course teachers, check the faculty page.
    (D) Detroit has plenty of accommodations available for out-of-town students.

11. (A) upon   (B) even after   (C) then   (D) following

12. (A) investments   (B) economics   (C) money   (D) finances

Part 7

Reading Comprehension

Select the best answer for each question and mark the letter (A), (B), (C), or (D).

Questions 13-14 refer to the following website.

http://www.indianasouth.edu

Your story at Indiana South University begins now

If you're considering applying to Indiana South University (ISU), this page is for you. We'll guide you through what's required, important deadlines, how to submit your application, and more.

Are you only just beginning to think about what happens after high school? We can help you start planning for college.

Freshman applicants

See freshman admission standards, application requirements, and tips on how to submit a strong application.

Transfer applicants

Learn how to transfer from your college to ISU and find out how your course credits may transfer.

Military/Veteran applicants

Read more about how to apply and special services and requirements for veterans.

International applicants

If you're applying from a country outside the United States, you'll want to visit the Office of International Services website. It will have useful information and resources to help make your admission process as smooth as possible.

13. **What is the purpose of this website?**

   (A) To inform potential applicants

   (B) To provide a history of the school

   (C) To compare admission fees

   (D) To show how to transfer to another school

14. **Who are NOT the target readers for this website?**

   (A) Freshman applicants

   (B) International applicants

   (C) Veteran applicants

   (D) Graduate applicants

"Storytelling in Education" by Robert Hill

To be a storyteller is an incredible opportunity to influence people, and each one of us has the ability to utilize storytelling in our classes. This book offers unique and powerful insights into how stories and storytelling can be utilized within higher education. Stories can shape our perspective of the world around us and be a useful tool for understanding concepts which tend to be difficult. —[1]—.

The conscious use of storytelling in higher education is not new, although less common in some academic areas. This book offers the opportunity to explore the concept of storytelling as an educational tool regardless of the subject area. —[2]—.

The book is based on the author's own experiences of using stories within teaching, from a story of "the Ecology of Law" to the exploration of accounting and finance through contemporary movies. Practical advice in each chapter ensures that ideas may be put into practice with ease. —[3]—.

In addition, the book also explores wider uses of storytelling for communication and ways of assessing student work. It also offers research insights, for example the question of whether positive stories of climate change have an impact on changing the behavior of readers more than negative stories. —[4]—.

15. What is true from this passage?

   (A) Storytelling is a new educational method.
   (B) Storytelling is sometime misleading.
   (C) Storytelling is useful for many subjects.
   (D) Storytelling is more effective for elderly people.

16. What is inferred about Robert Hill?

   (A) He was a movie director.
   (B) He was a teacher.
   (C) He was an environmentalist.
   (D) He was an accountant.

17 In which of the positions marked [1], [2], [3], and [4] does the following sentence best belong?

   "The various outcomes of the research examples will surprise most readers."

   (A) [1]   (C) [3]
   (B) [2]   (D) [4]

Daily Life

Select the best answer to complete the sentence. Then choose the letter (A), (B), (C), or (D).

1. The Volunteer Center collects information ------- to various courses offered by its member groups.

   (A) relative   (B) relation   (C) related   (D) relating

2. We have to choose an ------- sized air conditioner for our house.

   (A) increasingly   (B) appropriately   (C) unexpectedly   (D) extensively

3. The Thai restaurant that opened this month ------- its meals anywhere within three miles.

   (A) delivers   (B) goes   (C) faces   (D) handles

4. This is a smartphone application that can ------- the dimensions of the room you're in.

   (A) size   (B) measure   (C) post   (D) instruct

5. A reliable water supply is ------- necessary to help residents if there's a disaster.

   (A) absolute   (B) absoluteness   (C) absolutes   (D) absolutely

6. The train was delayed due to the ------- weather.

   (A) positive   (B) dark   (C) inclement   (D) essential

7. I got ------- traffic, and it took me an hour when it would have been 15 minutes otherwise.

   (A) managed to   (B) reached for   (C) along with   (D) stuck in

8. According to the survey, hybrid cars may eventually ------- cars that run on gasoline.

   (A) reinvest   (B) reuse   (C) replace   (D) reinvent

Text Completion

Select the best answer to complete the text. Then choose the letter (A), (B), (C), or (D).

Questions 9-12 refer to the following notice.

New Glasgow City has plans to convert all trails in this section of the park to mountain bike only trails. Trails will be controlled and ------ by the New Glasgow
9.
Mountain Biking Association (NGMBA). Runners, hikers, dog walkers and families will ------ be allowed to enjoy these trails. If you do not want these trails
10.
------ to mountain bike only trails, do something about it! ------. Your views on
11.   12.
this matter are important, so make sure they are heard.

9. (A) nurtured   (B) supplied   (C) maintained   (D) saved

10. (A) not at all   (B) no means   (C) negatively   (D) no longer

11. (A) convert   (B) converted   (C) converting   (D) have been converted

12. (A) Call City Hall to voice your opinion.
    (B) NGMBA has been around for over 10 years.
    (C) For hiking recommendations, please visit the City's website.
    (D) Discover a new way to enjoy and experience nature.

Reading Comprehension

Select the best answer for each question and mark the letter (A), (B), (C), or (D).

Questions 13-14 refer to the following report.

A recent survey of the reading and book-buying habits of young adults in the city has shown some changing attitudes towards reading. The survey, conducted by The Better Book Association, divided readers into four different groups:

Avid readers: They love reading and buying books, and tend to be well educated.

Money-conscious readers: They respond to discounts, and tend to be female or retired.

Impulse readers: They are light readers and tend to prefer less expensive books.

Reluctant readers: They prefer TV or social media that requires less concentration, and tend to have lower education.

Half of the young adults in the city read nearly every day and 1/4 go to bookstores once a month. Their buying habits are usually influenced by word of mouth rather than book reviews. The more avid readers are from a high socioeconomic class.

13. **What kind of readers are considered not well educated?**

(A) Avid readers

(B) Money-conscious readers

(C) Impulse readers

(D) Reluctant readers

14. **What often helps a person decide what book to buy?**

(A) A higher education

(B) A book review

(C) A person's recommendation

(D) A bookstore sale

Questions 15-17 refer to the following article.

Blue Circle Corp. has developed the world's first adult diapers designed to help elderly people with walking difficulties move more easily. The product, to go on sale Feb. 14, addresses a market need spurred on by the nation's rapidly graying population. The domestic adult diaper market has been growing at an annual rate of 5 percent and is expected to expand.

The diaper's effectiveness was confirmed based on the ease with which users raised their legs and the lengthening of their steps, according to Blue Circle, which has developed the product in collaboration with the Kentucky University of Health Sciences. "It appears that the diaper helps the wearer stand straighter," said Wendy Lawson, a professor of orthopedic and sports physical therapy at the university's School of Rehabilitation. "Being able to move on their own improves their quality of life," Lawson said.

Blue Circle's newest product is priced at $14 for a pack of 18 medium-sized diapers for those with a waist size of 60 to 85 centimeters or 16 large-size diapers for those with a waist size of 75-100 cm.

15. Who might be most interested in this article?

(A) Elderly people with weak eyesight

(B) Elderly people with leg trouble

(C) Elderly people with mental issues

(D) Elderly people with verbal difficulty

16. The word "graying" in paragraph 1, line 4, is closest in meaning to

(A) aging

(B) ambiguous

(C) growing

(D) middle

17. Who is Ms. Wendy Lawson?

(A) A corporate executive

(B) A university professor

(C) A helper for elderly people

(D) A diaper distributor

Health

Incomplete Sentences

Select the best answer to complete the sentence. Then choose the letter (A), (B), (C), or (D).

1. You ------- do more exercise if you're concerned about your weight.

   (A) have yet to (B) intend to (C) manage to (D) ought to

2. Modern medical technology is ------- developed, giving you many treatment options.

   (A) highly (B) high (C) higher (D) highs

3. MaxPro running machines are ------- well designed that they are guaranteed for fifteen years.

   (A) so (B) such (C) as (D) just

4. Walking is ideal for people who lack exercise ------- athletes who'd like to recharge their body.

   (A) but (B) either (C) as well as (D) additionally

5. AAA Fitness Club can check your blood pressure ------- you are not a member.

   (A) even if (B) along with (C) so that (D) while

6. The brochures sent by the childcare department describe the positive effects of ------- contact for youngsters.

   (A) physicality (B) physics (C) physically (D) physical

7. ------- a fraction of the lessons provided at Ogden Fitness can be seen on their website.

   (A) Only (B) Less (C) Enough (D) Very

8. Most medical emergencies happen -------, so you should always have health information on hand.

   (A) moderately (B) increasingly (C) suddenly (D) extensively

Text Completion

Select the best answer to complete the text. Then choose the letter (A), (B), (C), or (D).

Questions 9-12 refer to the following internal memo.

Good afternoon Solar World employees,

Once again, the city marathon application deadline is upon us. For the past seven years, Solar World has been able to ------ a five-member team to represent the company. In some years, we've had more than five people apply **9.** and in other years we've struggled to put together a team. I'd like to remind you all that this is a charity event and that ------ will be directed towards the team's **10.** charity of choice. Team members will also receive an additional 3 days-off ------ **11.** time spent training and practicing for the marathon. Those interested in joining should talk to Kelly in the Design Department who has once again volunteered to be the marathon team captain.

12.

Clark Kent

Solar World President

9. (A) collect   (B) group   (C) meet   (D) assemble

10. (A) pay   (B) funds   (C) proceeds   (D) assets

11. (A) to cover   (B) for instance   (C) instead of   (D) deal with

12. (A) I hope that we will finally win the city marathon.
    (B) Let's show the community the power of Solar World staff!
    (C) A list of possible charities will be given out at a later date.
    (D) Please reply explaining why you will or won't join this event.

Select the best answer for each question and mark the letter (A), (B), (C), or (D).

Questions 13-15 refer to the following article.

Everybody wants to look good and feel great. Getting into shape requires exercise, and in today's consumer culture, that often translates into dollars. However, that should not be the case.

Fitness is not something we can buy like new car or new clothes. Fitness only requires will power and a few basic items like running shoes or a bicycle. Many people follow their decision to get back into shape with a trip to the mall to buy exercise outfits and shoes that can cost hundreds of dollars. Some people buy fitness-training equipment while others spend heavily on health club memberships.

While some of these purchases may help someone get into shape, there is much exercise equipment that goes unused and takes up garage space. Likewise, there are untold numbers of unused gym memberships. Therefore, if you do make the decision to start exercising, start slowly, both physically and economically. If you jog, you can find a good pair of running shoes for 30-40 dollars. If you join a club, try a trial membership.

Before you make that big purchase for fitness, make sure you have the will power to get in shape first.

13. **What is the main idea of this article?**

    (A) People should exercise all the time.

    (B) Getting in shape costs a lot of money.

    (C) Health clubs offer great deals.

    (D) Exercise could be inexpensive.

14. **What does the author think of exercise equipment?**

    (A) It's economical.

    (B) It's sometimes helpful.

    (C) It's difficult to use regularly.

    (D) It's not necessary at all.

15. **What advice does the author give about gym memberships?**

    (A) Go as much as possible

    (B) Try a temporary membership first

    (C) Find an economical membership plan

    (D) Join the most popular gym

Questions 16-17 refer to the following website.

 http://www.mshospital.com

Miami State Hospital

Miami State Hospital remains open at this time. We have launched a virtual clinic to offer individuals in free screenings for the new virus on the virtual care mobile app. If you are experiencing symptoms or are concerned you may have the virus, we recommend using this virtual clinic.

Information on new virus

Learn more about the new virus, including FAQs and what you can do to help protect yourself and your family. View new virus information.

Visitor Restrictions

Our facilities have implemented visitor restrictions to help minimize the spread of the new virus, flu, and other diseases. View visitor restrictions.

16. What is the purpose of this hospital website?

   (A) To maximize its capacity
   (B) To minimize its costs and expenses
   (C) To manage a problem effectively
   (D) To change its old facilities

17. What is recommend for those who may have the new virus?

   (A) Report to the hospital ASAP
   (B) Consult with their home doctor
   (C) Use the virtual care mobile app
   (D) Don't panic and remain in bed

Job Interviews

Part 5

Incomplete Sentences

Select the best answer to complete the sentence. Then choose the letter (A), (B), (C), or (D).

1. We intend to ------- staff with expertise in financial services.

   (A) resign   (B) hope   (C) invest   (D) hire

2. The ------- candidate will have the ability to contribute greatly to our firm.

   (A) success   (B) successful   (C) successfully   (D) succeed

3. He has ------- as someone who can motivate employees.

   (A) editorials   (B) credentials   (C) catalogs   (D) directories

4. Many enterprises are paying attention to the communication abilities of ------- applicants.

   (A) dramatic   (B) typical   (C) dominant   (D) potential

5. Workers who ------- for more than eight years are eligible for a managerial promotion.

   (A) have worked   (B) working   (C) have been worked   (D) be worked

6. Employers would like to know if applicants prefer to work in a team or -------.

   (A) definitely   (B) flexibly   (C) independently   (D) mutually

7. ------- computerized information networks are growing, our company rapidly needs to increase engineers.

   (A) Although   (B) Instead   (C) Now that   (D) Meanwhile

8. ------- the instructions provided by Human Resources, all candidates were asked the same questions.

   (A) In the event that   (B) In accordance with   (C) In order that   (D) In front of

Text Completion

Select the best answer to complete the text. Then choose the letter (A), (B), (C), or (D).

Questions 9-12 refer to the following letter.

Dear Rick,

We regret to inform you at this time that you have not been selected for the position of Art Director at Cloud Tower. ------ our interview team, we appreciate
9.
the time you spent preparing for the interview and in coming to our offices.

------, we believe we have selected the candidate whom we believe most
10.
closely matches the job requirements of the position. If you would like more detailed feedback about your interview results, please feel free to let us know.

We enjoyed talking with you and especially appreciated the fact that you took
------ time with your application and interview. Bringing design ideas for some
11.
of our current clients showed the sort of proactive attitude we were looking for.

------. We also would like to thank you for your interest in our company.
12.

Sincerely,

Taylor Smith

---

9. (A) Instead of   (B) In part of   (C) On behalf of   (D) On duty

10. (A) In the end   (B) Additionally   (C) Sooner or later   (D) As you know

11. (A) noticeable   (B) reasonable   (C) respectable   (D) considerable

12. (A) Please let us know when you can begin working for us.

    (B) We wish you success with your continuing job search.

    (C) You will soon receive an e-mail about the time of the second interview.

    (D) I am glad that we could give you this good news.

Select the best answer for each question and mark the letter (A), (B), (C), or (D).

Questions 13-15 refer to the following notice.

Help Wanted!

Looking for people who are team players and love music.
Want to work in a dynamic retail environment?

Landmark Music is opening a new outlet in the Yorkville Mall Shopping Center. We are looking for high school graduates, preferably with some retail industry experience. Landmark Music is a national retailer with outlets in 18 states around the country. There are also career advancement opportunities for employees wishing to move into management positions.

Landmark Music is an equal opportunity employer.
Those who are interested should call 1-555-4568.

---

13. Who is encouraged to apply for this job?

   (A) People who enjoy working on their own
   (B) High school students who want to work part-time
   (C) People with some experience in retail
   (D) People with experience as musicians

14. Where is the new store located?

   (A) In a shopping center
   (B) On a university campus
   (C) On a street corner
   (D) In a department store

15. What should people who want to get this job do?

   (A) Go to the head office
   (B) E-mail the manager
   (C) Send a resume to the shop
   (D) Make a telephone call

To Whom It May Concern:

My name is Tom Stevens, and I run a private English language school. Ms. Nagisa Sato worked as my assistant for three years, preparing materials, and scheduling our classes. She was always well organized, and her attitude with our students was always professional, as well as amicable. She is a very reliable person, a fast learner, capable of doing administrative work, and on top of everything, has a good command of English. I highly recommend her for the position she is applying for. Please contact me if you would like more information.

Sincerely,

Tom Stevens

Tom Stevens
ABCDEnglish

16. What is the purpose of this letter?
   (A) To apply for a job position
   (B) To decline a job offer
   (C) To recommend a candidate
   (D) To apologize for a staff member

17. Who would most likely be the recipient of this letter?
   (A) The president of a company
   (B) The person in charge of recruiting
   (C) The director of finance
   (D) The applicant's current manager

Meetings

Part 5

Incomplete Sentences

Select the best answer to complete the sentence. Then choose the letter (A), (B), (C), or (D).

1. When we get ------- from our client, we will e-mail you the information.

   (A) allowance　　(B) transaction　　(C) confirmation　　(D) substance

2. This tool is to help you calculate the ------- cost of productivity loss.

   (A) approximately　(B) approximate　(C) approximating　(D) approximation

3. The new project will be started ------- the budget request has been approved.

   (A) in addition to　(B) by comparison　(C) as soon as　(D) at the same

4. Although the technical work needs to progress -------, sufficient time is required before the approval stage.

   (A) highly　　(B) timely　　(C) quickly　　(D) initially

5. He made ------- arrangements to accommodate clients who were unable to attend the meeting.

   (A) contrary　　(B) hastily　　(C) impolite　　(D) alternative

6. The committee advised us to increase productivity, ------- it means higher costs.

   (A) even if　　(B) except for　　(C) along with　　(D) in spite of

7. We should start by ------- business opportunities and finding entrepreneurs who would be able to run these businesses.

   (A) identified　　(B) identify　　(C) identifying　　(D) identifies

8. To come up ------- new innovations, it is essential for companies to encourage experimentation.

   (A) along　　(B) toward　　(C) with　　(D) in

Text Completion

Select the best answer to complete the text. Then choose the letter (A), (B), (C), or (D).

Questions 9-12 refer to the following memo.

To all staff,

Today's meeting will last longer than usual because we have so much to discuss. ------, we'll try and squeeze in a short break around the halfway mark.
9.
------, we'd like to finish everything on the agenda by 4:00.
10.

Meeting reminders:

· If you'll be absent or late for any reason, please tell Mark, marksmith@ liveevents.com

· Bring your laptop computer or tablet to access additional online information.

· Sit in your ------ seat according to the seating chart on the screen.
11.

One more thing: we have been asked by the cleaning staff to try and leave the meeting room the way we found it, i.e., clean. Apparently, there are plenty of coffee spills and stains after our meetings. If you plan to drink coffee during the meeting, like me, have something on hand to wipe up messes. ------.
12.

See you all at 1:30!

Amy Wilson

---

9. (A) Conversely   (B) Additionally   (C) To be exact   (D) As a result

10. (A) Ideally   (B) Partially   (C) Excellently   (D) Effectively

11. (A) assign   (B) assignment   (C) assigned   (D) assigning

12. (A) Coffee will be available in the cafeteria all day.
    (B) The cleaning staff would like me to thank you in advance.
    (C) Please strictly observe the rules of this office.
    (D) Thank the people who make these meetings a success.

Reading Comprehension

Select the best answer for each question and mark the letter (A), (B), (C), or (D).

Questions 13-14 refer to the following memorandum.

FROM: David Kim

TO: Local Branch Managers

RE: Annual HR Conference

Our annual HR Conference will be held at the Castle Hotel in Tokyo on March 3 and 4. After holding the meeting in Sapporo and then Fukuoka, we decided to move it to a venue in Tokyo, near our head office. This will minimize overall transportation and administrative costs for organizers.

I am looking forward to seeing you there.
Thank you.

David Kim

13. What is indicated about the location of this year's meeting?

    (A) It will be the same as previous years.

    (B) It will be easy for anyone from Sapporo to attend.

    (C) It will be easy for anyone from Fukuoka to attend.

    (D) It will reduce total costs for the company.

14. What is inferred from this memo?

    (A) All HR staff will get together.

    (B) Local branch managers will attend this meeting.

    (C) A conference call will be held.

    (D) The company is located within the Castle Hotel.

TO: All Department Heads
FROM: Dennis Fung
RE: New Benefit System Meetings

Please make sure your staff is aware of their designated meeting time slots regarding our company's new benefit system that goes into effect next month. Susan Rodriguez, HR Director, will manage the meetings in Conference Room A on the 11th floor.

Accounting 10:00-11:00
Marketing 11:10-12:10
Research and Development.... 14:00-15:00
Sales 15:30-16:30
Other administrative staff 17:00-18:00

Refreshments will be available for those in the last meeting time slot. Employees unable to attend their department's designated time must contact Stephanie in HR to arrange to attend another time slot that day.

Thank you for your attention,

Dennis Fung
HR Manager

15. **What is the main purpose of this meeting?**

   (A) To schedule a meeting time

   (B) To change the budget for benefit plans

   (C) To inform people of refreshments

   (D) To learn about the new benefit system

16. **Why would someone need to talk to Stephanie?**

   (A) To make an appointment for the meeting

   (B) To transfer to another department

   (C) To change their scheduled meeting slot

   (D) To select something from the dinner menu

17. **Who will be provided with refreshments?**

   (A) All administrative staff

   (B) All attendees

   (C) Employees who are busy working

   (D) Those who attend the last meeting

Money

Part 5

Incomplete Sentences

Select the best answer to complete the sentence. Then choose the letter (A), (B), (C), or (D).

1. The exchange ------- are updated according to fluctuations of the global economy.

   (A) deals   (B) ratios   (C) parts   (D) rates

2. We are concerned with how economists ------- the costs and benefits of the new virus lockdowns.

   (A) calculate   (B) calculating   (C) been calculated   (D) calculates

3. EED Inc. decided to invest a ------- amount of money in plant modernization.

   (A) quite   (B) much   (C) substantial   (D) many

4. ------- ability to pay, we offer a variety of services to suit everyone.

   (A) Furthermore   (B) Assuming that   (C) Regardless of   (D) Subsequently

5. Strong strategic-thinking ------- and sharp marketing instincts are important qualities for a successful product manager.

   (A) skills   (B) findings   (C) realities   (D) approximations

6. The DSD Bank has specialized in ------- money since last year.

   (A) remittance   (B) remitting   (C) remits   (D) remit

7. That cash is ------- a payment option makes our parking experience easier, simpler, and faster.

   (A) either   (B) no longer   (C) once   (D) since

8. It may be difficult to ------- wealth right after graduation.

   (A) arrange   (B) assume   (C) accomplish   (D) accumulate

Text Completion

Select the best answer to complete the text. Then choose the letter (A), (B), (C), or (D).

Questions 9-12 refer to the following article.

Choosing People to Appear on Paper Currencies

As with the nation's coins, the Secretary of the Treasury usually selects the designs shown on the United States paper currency. US law ------ portraits of
9.
living persons from appearing on money. ------, the portraits on US currency
10.
notes are of deceased persons whose places in history is known well by the American people.

The basic face and back designs of all amounts of US paper currency in circulation today were selected in 1928 by a committee. ------. It depicts the
11.
eye and the pyramid found in the Great Seal of the United States and was put on the reverse of the one-dollar note in 1935 by a separate committee.

Unfortunately, US records do not suggest why certain presidents and statesmen ------ for specific denominations, like the smaller one-dollar and five-
12.
dollar bills.

---

9. (A) enacts   (B) executes   (C) performs   (D) prohibits

10. (A) Therefore   (B) After all   (C) Anyway   (D) Though

11. (A) The designs of currency notes are usually decided by the President.
    (B) The only exception is the reverse design of the one-dollar bill.
    (C) The more famous a person was, the higher the currency note they were on.
    (D) The most acclaimed design was the 100-dollar note with Ben Franklin's image.

12. (A) choose   (B) chose   (C) chosen   (D) were chosen

Select the best answer for each question and mark the letter (A), (B), (C), or (D).

Questions 13-14 refer to the following letter.

September 23

Dear Mr. Orland,

This is your third and final reminder that your account of 1,765 dollars is past due. This account is in regard to the purchase and delivery of the following.

Item	Amount
Deep fryer	1
Dish washer	1
Wine fridges	2

This account has been past due since April 25. If payment is not received by October 24, we will have no alternative but to turn your account over to a collection agency. Accounts placed with a collection agency may damage your credit history and affect your credibility to establish new lines of credit for the next five years. Once this account is turned over to a collection agency, you may be required to pay subsequent legal and court costs which may exceed the amount owned.

Awaiting your prompt response to this matter.

Sincerely,

John Smith

John Smith
General Manager
Milwaukee Restaurant Supply

13. What is the purpose of this letter?

  (A) To apologize for an incorrect invoice
  (B) To inquire about equipment prices
  (C) To cancel a recent order
  (D) To notify of outstanding debt

14. How long has this account been active?

  (A) One month
  (B) Three months
  (C) Six months
  (D) A year

Questions 15-17 refer to the following website.

 http://www.islandbank.com

Island Bank

Headquartered in Port Louis, Mauritius, Island Bank is a universal bank serving four main banking segments: consumer, corporate, private, and international. Island Bank provides a wide range of banking products to its clients through a chain of 13 branches and a well-distributed ATM network across the island. It also offers treasury services and has developed strong capabilities in e-commerce. It was awarded "Best Bank in E-Commerce Business Risk Management" by *London Economist* for 2018.

Besides this, Island Bank is licensed by the Financial Services Commission as an insurance agent, distributor of financial products, and investment advisor. Island Bank also has a representative office in South Africa.

Island Bank has shareholders owning sizeable banking operations in Madagascar, Kenya, Tanzania, and Rwanda. Undeniably, it is one of the few banks in Mauritius to have a tangible presence in Africa and is strategically positioned to benefit from local market insight and the vast market potential of the continent. It aims to offer the Island Bank advantage to clients looking to invest or establish a foothold in Africa.

15. Where is the location of Island Bank's main office?

(A) In Mauritius

(B) In Madagascar

(C) In Kenya

(D) In South Africa

16. What is NOT a business function of this bank?

(A) Consumer banking

(B) Corporate auditing

(C) Insurance

(D) Finance advising

17. What is suggested on this website?

(A) Island Bank is the leading bank in Africa.

(B) Island Bank was originally established in South Africa.

(C) Island Bank is a gateway to invest in Africa.

(D) Island Bank is exclusive to Port Louis, Mauritius.

Scene **8**

Office Life

Incomplete Sentences

Select the best answer to complete the sentence. Then choose the letter (A), (B), (C), or (D).

1. I'd be really ------- of any information you can tell me.

   (A) appreciated   (B) appreciate   (C) appreciative (D) appreciation

2. Although they were transferred to different branches, they ------- with one another.

   (A) kept in touch   (B) looked forward (C) took back   (D) watched out

3. I was in ------- of that issue and eventually corresponded with my predecessor.

   (A) charge   (B) room   (C) part   (D) supervision

4. Our employees can use the ABC gym for free through a special agreement ------- our parent company.

   (A) in   (B) about   (C) for   (D) with

5. ------- of our company on TV is a very valuable way to promote our brands.

   (A) Having exposed (B) Being exposed (C) Expose   (D) Exposure

6. ------- our company just started a few months ago, I believe we'll soon dominate the market.

   (A) Besides   (B) Whenever   (C) Although   (D) If

7. After understanding why the error occurred, you can then ------- the cause of the problem.

   (A) assure   (B) address   (C) regret   (D) transform

8. As a researcher, Miyako is ------- qualified to present the results of this survey.

   (A) uniquely   (B) sharply   (C) severely   (D) approximately

Text Completion

Select the best answer to complete the text. Then choose the letter (A), (B), (C), or (D).

Questions 9-12 refer to the following article.

Today, the modern company has access to options beyond the traditional office setting. More companies are ------ work-from-home arrangements for their
9.
employees, and many organizations are turning to video conferencing tools. These apps provide many benefits. ------. One concern is where uninvited
10.
guests attend video conference meetings simply by accessing meeting IDs. While this might seem like a minor ------, it could turn into a major issue if the
11.
meeting involves highly sensitive and confidential information. ------, they can
12.
also use the chat portion of these tools to spread malicious links or upload files.

9. (A) implementing   (B) outsourcing   (C) acquiring   (D) assigning

10. (A) Problems and concerns with these tools are very minimal, to say the least.
    (B) These benefits are what make companies so happy to use these apps.
    (C) However, they present the challenge of ensuring that employees and data remain secure.
    (D) It must be said, though, that the annual fees for these tools is usually quite expensive.

11. (A) anger   (B) comfort   (C) achievement (D) annoyance

12. (A) Consequently (B) Anyway   (C) Additionally (D) Finally

Reading Comprehension

Select the best answer for each question and mark the letter (A), (B), (C), or (D).

Questions 13-15 refer to the following notice.

Attention Employees!

Recently, there have been a rash of car thefts in the employee parking lot. Last year, there were 16 reported auto thefts and an additional 23 break-ins where personal items left in cars were stolen. Security has been beefed up, and although an arrest was made six weeks ago. It appears the problem has not gone away.

Therefore, management, while trying to do everything we can to stop these thefts and break-ins, is asking employees to do the following:

1) Roll up your windows, lock your doors and always set your car alarm if you have one installed.
2) Do not leave valuables in your car.
3) Report any suspicious persons and/or behavior in the parking lot to security immediately.

Lastly, there is a 5,000-dollar reward to anyone providing information (no questions asked) leading to the conviction of any suspects.

13. How many cars were stolen last year?

(A) 12

(B) 16

(C) 23

(D) 30

14. Where have the thefts taken place?

(A) In a shopping center

(B) Along a residential block

(C) On a street

(D) In a company parking area

15. When will the money be awarded?

(A) When the thieves are convicted

(B) When the stolen cars are found

(C) When police are informed

(D) When the thieves are witnessed

Orange's Mike Sanders expands U.S. remote working offer to many global employees

Orange Inc. CEO Mike Sanders is offering employees at most of its global offices the ability to work from home, calling the new virus outbreak an "unprecedented event" and a "challenging moment." —[1]—.

Sanders told employees at several global offices to "please feel free to work remotely if your job allows" in March, according to a memo he sent. That extends the company's move last Friday, when it encouraged employees in California and New York City to work remotely. —[2]—.

This policy impacts "areas with the greatest density of infections," Sanders said, applying it to Orange's corporate offices in California, NYC, Hong Kong, Singapore, Japan, Italy, Germany, France, Switzerland, and the U.K. —[3]—.

Beyond encouraging work from home, Sanders said Orange is "making a major effort to reduce human density and ensure those teams that are on-site can do their work safely and with peace of mind."

Orange is implementing "new policies to maximize interpersonal space," according to the memo. —[4]—.

16. Why is Mike Sanders offering employees the chance to work from home?
    (A) To save on communing time
    (B) Due to limited office space
    (C) To encourage more family time
    (D) As protection against a health risk

17. What is inferred from the article about Orange?
    (A) The California and NYC locations are in danger.
    (B) The CEO lives and works in New York City.
    (C) The corporate offices are exclusively located in America.
    (D) It will encourage employees to work closely with colleagues.

18. In which of the positions [1], [2], [3], and [4] does the following sentence best belong?
    "These efforts include reducing human density and occupancy at Orange stores around the world."
    (A) [1]   (B) [2]   (C) [3]   (D) [4]

Recreation

Part 5

Incomplete Sentences

Select the best answer to complete the sentence. Then choose the letter (A), (B), (C), or (D).

1. Admission for two adult guardians accompanying children will be ------- by half.

   (A) expected   (B) added   (C) reduced   (D) took

2. The swimming center ------- an abundance of grass and shaded areas for picnics.

   (A) featuring   (B) features   (C) was featured   (D) feature

3. Most parents ------- enjoyment from watching their children play sports.

   (A) admire   (B) behave   (C) derive   (D) perform

4. The website advises users to review their reservations carefully as it is difficult to change ------- the date is confirmed.

   (A) but   (B) once   (C) right away   (D) by means of

5. The special exhibition will be held for five ------- days.

   (A) inconsecutive   (B) consecutiveness   (C) consecutively   (D) consecutive

6. Personal fitness trainers assist members, tailoring the programs to ------- individual's needs.

   (A) each   (B) all   (C) some   (D) many

7. The Museum of Art announced changes in its admission fees that will go into ------- on October 1.

   (A) effect   (B) effected   (C) effectiveness   (D) effective

8. ------- experiencing the tea ceremony you can learn about Japanese culture.

   (A) Beside   (B) Due to   (C) Despite   (D) Through

Part 6

Text Completion

Select the best answer to complete the text. Then choose the letter (A), (B), (C), or (D).

Questions 9-12 refer to the following web page.

The Colorado Hiking Association (CHA) believes that being in nature has a positive ------ on people's hearts, minds, and bodies. It is vital for everyone to
9.
have the opportunity to access the outdoors, and we are committed to reducing barriers to hiking trails and lands. We strive to inspire people to go outside, giving them the skills and knowledge they need to enjoy themselves ------. Our
10.
voice is ------ by the support of our members and every volunteer who helps to
11.
build and maintain trails. ------.
12.

9. (A) shock   (B) feeling   (C) encounter   (D) impact

10. (A) carefully   (B) fully   (C) partially   (D) exactly

11. (A) strong   (B) strongest   (C) strength   (D) strengthened

12. (A) Call us today to reserve the hiking trail of your choice.
    (B) For current area weather conditions, click here.
    (C) Join us by becoming an active CHA member today.
    (D) To report a problem on one of the trails, follow these instructions.

Reading Comprehension

Select the best answer for each question and mark the letter (A), (B), (C), or (D).

Questions 13-14 refer to the following notice.

The Florida Aquarium is a fantastic place to take your kids on any weekday. That's because kids are now half-price from Monday to Friday. So avoid the weekend crowds. With over 200 different species of sea creatures. The Florida Aquarium is the place to be.

	Weekdays	**Sat-Sun & Holidays**
Opening Hours	9:00 a.m.- 6:00 p.m.	10:00 a.m. – 6:00 p.m.
	Adults/Children (ages 4-12)	Adults/Children (ages 4-12)
Admission	$20/$5	$20/$10

13. Why is going to this aquarium on a weekday recommended?

   (A) Penguin shows are only on weekdays.

   (B) Children can enter at a cheaper price.

   (C) A free gift is given.

   (D) Children can attend a workshop.

14. How much would admission cost for one parent and their 3 and 8-year-old children on Friday?

   (A) $25

   (B) $35

   (C) $45

   (D) $55

Questions 15-16 refer to the following website.

 http://www.y20ticket.com/info

The Youthful 20 Ticket is a seasonally available railway ticket, which gives you six days of unlimited, nationwide travel on local and rapid trains for only 12,000 yen, or 2,400 yen per day!

Availability: The Youthful 20 Ticket is only available three times a year during school holiday seasons, as shown in the table below:

Period	Valid	On Sale
Spring	March 5 to April 5	February 20 to March 1
Summer	July 25 to September 5	June 25 to August 31
Winter	December 15 to January 5	December 1 to December 27

Eligibility: Despite its name, the Youthful 20 Ticket can be used by people of any age. It is available to foreign tourists as well as Japanese nationals and foreign residents of Japan. However, there is no special reduced fare for children.

15. Which of the following times can someone purchase this ticket?

(A) Year-round

(B) March 5

(C) June 20

(D) February 25

16. The word "Eligibility" in line 10 is closest in meaning to

(A) exemption

(B) qualification

(C) reliability

(D) dependability

Restaurants

Part 5

Incomplete Sentences

Select the best answer to complete the sentence. Then choose the letter (A), (B), (C), or (D).

1. The chef served a vegetarian dish for the customer ------- the last-minute request.

   (A) respond   (B) despite   (C) beyond   (D) aside

2. Mr. Tsuji plans to host the reception ------- promoting Japanese food culture.

   (A) to   (B) for   (C) at   (D) in

3. It is often said that ------- vegetables are good for your health.

   (A) steam   (B) steaming   (C) steamed   (D) steams

4. The Happy Fisherman is glad to ------- you up on crab cakes and other seafood specialties.

   (A) satisfy   (B) fill   (C) treat   (D) eat

5. We decided to send out meal coupons thanking customers for their ------- patronage.

   (A) loyal   (B) long   (C) modest   (D) content

6. White truffles are one of the most ------- appreciated ingredients in French cooking.

   (A) lightly   (B) rapidly   (C) shortly   (D) highly

7. We guarantee that our salads are fresher than ------- of our competitors.

   (A) which   (B) them   (C) what   (D) those

8. The event was held to honor Food Award recipients while ------- the area's image.

   (A) enhancing   (B) to enhance   (C) has enhanced   (D) enhance

Part 6

Text Completion

Select the best answer to complete the text. Then choose the letter (A), (B), (C), or (D).

Questions 9-12 refer to the following advertisement.

Restaurant2Go is an easy way to get the food you love delivered to your home or office. Download the Restaurant2Go app and ------ from hundreds of
9.
restaurants. When you find something you like, tap to add it to your cart. When you're ready to check out, you'll see your address, an ------ delivery time, and
10.
the price of the order including tax and delivery fee. If everything looks fine, just tap "Place order." ------, when the order's almost ready, a Restaurant2Go
11.
representative will go to the restaurant to pick it up. Next, they'll bring it to you. You'll be able to see their name and photo and track their progress all on the Restaurant2Go app. ------
12.

9. (A) to choose   (B) choosing   (C) choose   (D) will choose

10. (A) effective   (B) efficient   (C) estimated   (D) inclusive

11. (A) Then   (B) However   (C) In addition (D) Therefore

12. (A) The quickest way to make restaurant reservations.
    (B) Ordering takeout has never been so easy!
    (C) You'll never take another taxi again.
    (D) You'll receive easy to make meals in minutes.

Reading Comprehension

Select the best answer for each question and mark the letter (A), (B), (C), or (D).

Questions13-14 refer to the following menu.

Kaya's Sandwich Shop

Hours: Mon-Fri: 10 a.m.-9 p.m. Sat & Sun: 11 a.m.-7 p.m.

Take-out Menu

Meat Sandwiches (all sandwiches come complete with vegetables and condiments of your choice):

Beef Salami Italiano $6.95	Chicken Breast............................$6.95
Romanian Pastrami................. $6.95	Breast of Turkey $6.95
Honey-cured Ham................... $6.95	Homemade Meatball $8.95
Thick-cut Bacon $6.95	

Vegetarian Sandwiches:

Baked Tofu.............................. $5.95	Plain Vegetable..............................$4.95

Combination Sandwiches (excludes meatball)
Any two meats, meat and tofu, or extra vegetables........................ $8.95
Any three items... $9.95

Sides:

Kaya's Crispy Potato Chips.... $2.00	Giant Polish Dill Pickle $2.00

Desserts:

Apple Pie $3.00	Chocolate Pudding $3.00

Soft Drink (Cola, Diet-Cola, Iced Tea, Lemonade, Ginger Ale, Orange Juice) ...$2.00

Lunch Special (Served Mon-Fri, 11 a.m.-2 p.m.)
Receive complimentary side, dessert, or soft drink with any sandwich purchase!

---

13. Which combination sandwich is NOT available?

    (A) Turkey and bacon

    (B) Bacon and meatball

    (C) Tofu, turkey, and salami

    (D) Tofu, chicken, and extra vegetables

14. Which time can you order a lunch special?

    (A) Monday 11:30 A.M.

    (B) Tuesday 3:00 P.M.

    (C) Friday 2:30 P.M.

    (D) Saturday 12:00 noon

Kimono Coffee to enter Viet Nam

Ho Chi Minh, Viet Nam - (Viet BUSINESS PRESS)—March 23

Kimono Coffee and Dung Enterprises today announced a joint agreement to open Kimono Coffee shops in Viet Nam.

Hiroshi Komoda, President of Kimono Coffee, expects the first Kimono Coffee shop to open in Ho Chi Minh in early July.

"The presence of Kimono in Viet Nam is, we feel, long overdue. The Viet Nam people love nothing better than a hot, strong cup of coffee in a pleasant setting, for a good price. Kimono provides all of these."

Besides Ho Chi Minh, Kimono is making plans to expand its outlets to other cities in Viet Nam later this year, while exploring further opportunities in South East Asia.

"Dung Enterprises has been the company we wanted to partner with since we began looking at the South East Asian market." said Takato Komoda, Kimono's Executive Director. "Not only do they have an innovative attitude, they also share our corporate philosophy and values."

Since going international in 2014, Kimono has opened coffee shops in six countries and has over 300 outlets in Japan, Taiwan, Hong Kong and America.

15. Why does Hiroshi Komoda think Kimono Coffee will succeed in Viet Nam?

    (A) It is successful everywhere.
    (B) The economy is very strong.
    (C) It can satisfy customers' needs.
    (D) It has many outlets.

16. How will Kimono Coffee operate in Viet Nam?

    (A) With several partners
    (B) Independently
    (C) The same way as in India
    (D) With a carefully selected partner

17. Which statement about Kimono Coffee is true?

    (A) They have many outlets in South East Asia.
    (B) They plan to open an outlet in India.
    (C) They will have outlets in South East Asia.
    (D) They have eight outlets in Viet Nam.

Scene **11**

Cooking

Part 5

Incomplete Sentences

Select the best answer to complete the sentence. Then choose the letter (A), (B), (C), or (D).

1. Farmers sell ------- produce to farmers' cooperatives or on wholesale markets.

   (A) them   (B) their   (C) they   (D) themselves

2. ------- just using it to reheat food, a microwave oven can be used for cooking.

   (A) Depending on (B) As far   (C) Based on   (D) Instead of

3. Foods that can be prepared and eaten ------- are labeled as "fast food."

   (A) aboard   (B) early   (C) quickly   (D) straight

4. You can add all the ------- at the same time to the mixing bowl.

   (A) tastes   (B) ingredients   (C) recipes   (D) groceries

5. We have many *daifuku* variations ------- include strawberry, beans, and ice cream.

   (A) what   (B) who   (C) which   (D) where

6. Try our easy recipes that are low in price but rich in -------.

   (A) nutrition   (B) economy   (C) mouth   (D) wallet

7. Japanese traditional dishes are ------- to match the pace at which people are eating.

   (A) had   (B) eaten   (C) ordered   (D) served

8. Supplements and energy drinks of Nutri Foods Inc. are produced in ------- factories.

   (A) separately   (B) separate   (C) separating   (D) separation

Text Completion

Select the best answer to complete the text. Then choose the letter (A), (B), (C), or (D).

Questions 9-12 refer to the following advertisement.

COOKE'S COOKBOOK FOR COOKS

Flamingo Publishing is proud to announce the release of celebrity chef Andrew Cooke's ------ anticipated first cookbook *Cooke's Cookbook for Cooks*.
9.

After years of working with the world's best chefs, Andrew opened the extremely successful Black Swan restaurant, which now boasts several locations around North America. Last year, Andrew ------ with Japanese chef
10.
Henry Suzuki to open TOCYO, the award-winning Japanese-American fusion restaurant in downtown Manhattan.

In *Cooke's Cookbook for Cooks*, Andrew goes step-by-step through some of his most ------ culinary creations. Each easy-to-make dish is accompanied by
11.
beautiful photography, to help you envision every unique recipe.

Alert!!! This is short notice, but Andrew Cooke will be promoting this book release by signing copies at Bordertown Books in Manhattan this Saturday, March 17, from 2 P.M. to 3 P.M. ------. Don't worry, another signing event is
12.
being planned for later this month. In the meantime, *Cooke's Cookbook for Cooks* is now available for pre-order! Visit flamingopublishing.com for details!

---

9. (A) quickly   (B) vaguely   (C) highly   (D) sincerely

10. (A) cooperated   (B) collected   (C) commenced   (D) collaborated

11. (A) success   (B) successful   (C) succeeding   (D) succeeded

12. (A) We understand some will be unable to attend this special event.
   (B) Ask chef Andrew to cook you one of his special dishes.
   (C) Reservations for TOCYO need to be made one month in advance.
   (D) Stop by Black Swan for something to eat after the signing event.

Part 7
Reading Comprehension

Select the best answer for each question and mark the letter (A), (B), (C), or (D).

Questions 13-17 refer to the following website and review.

https://www.15minuterecipes.com/readercontribution/macaroni-ham-pineapple-salad

Today's Reader Contribution:

Macaroni, Ham, & Pineapple Salad

from Jody Johnston

"I love this website and all the different dish ideas from ordinary people like me! So, here's my idea: a delicious macaroni salad that is so refreshing. I use ingredients I like and make it regularly during the summer to go with lunches or as a meal on a really hot day. It's also an easy recipe to modify according to your own preferences. Enjoy!" —*Jody*

Preparation time: 15 mins + 1hr refrigeration time
Servings: 5 people

Ingredients:

1 package of elbow macaroni

1 cup of Italian-style salad dressing

2 cans of crushed pineapple

1 ham steak, cut into cubes

2 stalks of celery, diced

2 plum tomatoes, diced

2 hard-boiled eggs, chopped

½ onion, diced

Directions:

  Step 1

Bring a large pot of salted water to a boil. Cook elbow macaroni in the boiling water, stirring occasionally until cooked through, 8 minutes; drain. Transfer hot macaroni to a large bowl.

  Step 2

Pour Italian-style salad dressing and crushed pineapple over the macaroni; stir. Add ham, celery, tomatoes, eggs, and onion; stir.

  Step 3

Cover bowl with plastic wrap and refrigerate until chilled, at least 1 hour.

Hillary Clifton

★★★★☆ *February 2*

A unique dish that I could make with little trouble. I did try an experiment. Rather than using pineapples, I substituted apples. This seemed to offer better texture and overall flavor. I also decided not to use celery, as my husband is not a fan. I have one small complaint, though. This site is devoted to dishes you can make in about 15 minutes or less. With the hour of refrigeration needed, I wonder if this recipe is appropriate or not. Adding the word "optional" to that step might make everyone happy.

Anyway, thanks for the great idea, Jody!

13. What is true about this website?

(A) It shows recipes from famous restaurants.

(B) It is for people who want vegetarian salad recipes.

(C) It allows readers to contribute their own ideas.

(D) It was created by Jody Johnston.

14. What is indicated about this recipe?

(A) It's possible to replace ingredients.

(B) It has many complicated steps.

(C) It takes nearly a full day to make.

(D) It can serve a dozen people.

15. What does Ms. Clifton say she did?

(A) Made the recipe with her husband

(B) Ate the dish by herself

(C) Substituted one ingredient

(D) Experimented with serving sizes

16. What was Ms. Clifton's complaint?

(A) The recipe was too troublesome.

(B) There were too many costly ingredients.

(C) The preparation time was too long.

(D) There are too many similar recipes.

17. In the review, the word "offer" in paragraph 1, line 2, is closest in meaning to

(A) promise something

(B) produce an effect

(C) propose an idea

(D) present for sale

Travel & Hotels 1

Incomplete Sentences

Select the best answer to complete the sentence. Then choose the letter (A), (B), (C), or (D).

1. We apologize for the ------- with all northbound trains.

   (A) belated　　　(B) overdue　　　(C) delay　　　(D) behind

2. Yun Performing Arts has been the world's ------- classical dance company for more than 30 years.

   (A) premiers　　　(B) premier　　　(C) premiership　　　(D) premiered

3. Normally we'd go through the South Trail, but a part of it is closed ------- maintenance today.

   (A) for　　　(B) in　　　(C) at　　　(D) of

4. Airport staff provide assistance for passengers ------- are ill or injured to assure a safe and comfortable trip.

   (A) where　　　(B) what　　　(C) which　　　(D) who

5. Train passes are refundable only if presented at a travel center designated to ------- them.

   (A) conduct　　　(B) handle　　　(C) submit　　　(D) pay

6. We provide a tour of the Grand Canyon that is historically -------.

   (A) informative　　　(B) inform　　　(C) information　　　(D) informs

7. The hotel is in the perfect ------- for easy access to all the most beautiful beaches.

   (A) venue　　　(B) location　　　(C) room　　　(D) placement

8. Guests staying in that ------- can enjoy a great view of the mountains.

   (A) direction　　　(B) stay　　　(C) accommodation　　　(D) manufacturer

Text Completion

Select the best answer to complete the text. Then choose the letter (A), (B), (C), or (D).

Questions 9-12 refer to the following e-mail.

Hello everyone,

As you know, this latest health crisis has affected many countries and their travel policies.

Here at One World Travel, we have been hard hit with many overseas travel cancellations from tour groups and individuals. Another problem is we do not know how long these changes and restrictions ------.
   9.

It goes without saying that this is affecting our bottom line. As president of the company, I am happy to say that your jobs are ------, and we will find a way out
   10.
of this situation together. We are one family at One World.

In the meantime, I would like to fill you in on some of our short-term projects. ------, beginning as early as next week, we will begin a print advertising
   11.
campaign focusing more on domestic travel destinations, highlighting areas of historical interest.

Your branch manager will be in touch with you in the next couple days to offer you a chance to participate in these exciting new assignments.

------.
   12.
Thank you for your hard work and dedication!

Steve Blanc
President, One World Travel

9. (A) last (B) lasts (C) lasted (D) will last

10. (A) serious (B) secure (C) risky (D) predictable

11. (A) However (B) On the contrary (C) For instance (D) Accordingly

12. (A) Your cooperation during this difficult time is necessary.
(B) We will notify you soon about temporary staff reductions.
(C) We will contact you about new overseas assignments.
(D) Please check our website for more details.

Part 7

Reading Comprehension

Select the best answer for each question and mark the letter (A), (B), (C), or (D).

Questions 13-17 refer to the following web page and e-mail.

● ● ●   https//www.bigislanddiving.com/instructors

| Home | Services | **Diving Instructors** | Contact |

At Big Island Diving, we have the friendliest most experience instructors in the business.

Jenny Suzuki (SCUBA for Advanced Divers)

Jenny has over 15 years experience and has been our Advanced SCUBA instructor for the past 4 years. No one on the island is more familiar with its deep-diving sites than Jenny. We're lucky to have her.

Alex Ovechkin (SCUBA for Beginners)

Alex began his diving career 10 years ago overseas in Thailand, then Bali, and now Hawaii. For the past 2 years, Alex has led our SCUBA beginner course and is one of our more popular instructors. Check out our school's reviews to see why.

Wyatt Johnston (Snorkeling for Adults)
Marie Johnston (Snorkeling for Kids)

We began our snorkeling course and tour just over a year ago. Led by the husband and wife team, Wyatt and Marie Johnston, these relaxing classes and tours are perfect for the swimmer who wants to try something new and exciting, but doesn't want to face too difficult a challenge. Kids and adults have separate classes (at the same time and in close proximity), but tours take place together. Fun for the whole family.

Note: due to unforeseen circumstances instructors may change.

From: clairewalker@bigislanddiving.com
To: janhooks@scubaworld.com
Date: June 11
Subject: instructor recommendation

Hey Jan,

I hope you're doing well and are all set for the upcoming tourist season. It looks like it'll be a busy one!

I'm actually e-mailing you today about a former diving instructor that used to work for you. One of our instructors is leaving soon, as she's expecting a baby, and we need to fill her position temporarily. We asked around and received the resume of Chad Summers. On it, he wrote that he had instructor experience at Scuba World. Also, if all goes well, he'd be in charge of our Advanced diving course and tour. It says he had been teaching high-level classes at Scuba World. Can you support this?

Anything else you can tell me about Chad would be appreciated.

Best regards,

Claire Walker

Big Island Diving

13. What is the purpose of this web page?

(A) To announce the opening of a new business

(B) To display job opportunities

(C) To provide information on personnel

(D) To accept reservations and reviews

14. What is true about Big Island Diving?

(A) It is based in Thailand.

(B) It caters exclusively to advanced divers.

(C) It was founded two years ago.

(D) It can accommodate families.

15. What is the purpose of the e-mail?

(A) To check the background of a candidate

(B) To look for some possible applicants

(C) To offer Ms. Hooks employment

(D) To ask for some business advice

16. Who will be taking temporary leave?

(A) Jenny Suzuki

(B) Wyatt Johnston

(C) Marie Johnston

(D) Claire Walker

17. In the e-mail, the word "support" in paragraph 2, line 6, is closest in meaning to?

(A) sustain   (C) confirm

(B) investigate   (D) strengthen

Office

Part 5

Incomplete Sentences

Select the best answer to complete the sentence. Then choose the letter (A), (B), (C), or (D).

1. Owing to his excellent work performance, he was ------- to lead the next new project.

   (A) persuading   (B) persuasion   (C) persuaded   (D) persuasively

2. That supplier always ------- our order when we're in a pinch.

   (A) accomplishes   (B) places   (C) accommodates   (D) sells

3. Please keep me in the ------- if any problems occur during your business trip.

   (A) line   (B) contact   (C) transaction   (D) loop

4. While Dave changed his computer recently, Henry has used ------- for about ten years.

   (A) himself   (B) his   (C) him   (D) he

5. Our meeting was ------- by the sudden construction noise in the building.

   (A) disrupted   (B) operated   (C) resisted   (D) implemented

6. He adjusted his busy schedule for us despite our ------- request.

   (A) conscious   (B) last-minute   (C) plenty of   (D) prolonged

7. ------- being a capable leader, we also think of her as a good colleague.

   (A) Besides   (B) However   (C) Despite   (D) Concerning

8. Due to a mail server -------, our mailing system was shut down this week.

   (A) response   (B) malfunction   (C) chaotic   (D) disorganized

Text Completion

Select the best answer to complete the text. Then choose the letter (A), (B), (C), or (D).

Questions 9-12 refer to the following web article.

A web application is like a phone app with the advantage that it's stored on the Internet and can perform on any Internet browser. A company would only have ------ the application once and then any employee could work with the
9.
application. This is really ------ for large companies with different branches,
10.
as well as for students, entrepreneurs and plenty of users who need certain programs but would rather avoid filling their computers with applications. ------.
11.
Large companies only have to solve a given issue once on the Internet browser, not address it on a one-by-one basis on every single computer. ------, other
12.
benefits of web apps are that there are no compatibility issues with operating systems and they don't take up space in a computer.

9. (A) install   (B) installing   (C) to install   (D) installed

10. (A) useless   (B) beneficial   (C) qualified   (D) proper

11. (A) A web application is also very easy to maintain.
    (B) Companies are also responsible for choosing the best plan.
    (C) Plus, phone apps are convenient as everyone has smart phones these days.
    (D) Also, people prefer face-to-face interactions.

12. (A) However   (B) In addition   (C) Yet   (D) After all

Part 7

Reading Comprehension

Select the best answer for each question and mark the letter (A), (B), (C), or (D).

Questions 13-17 refer to the following e-mail, web page and article.

From: jamescameron@bellevilleuniversity.com
To: SBA Faculty <sbafaculty@bellevilleuniversity.com>
Date: January 30
Subject: Distance Online Classes (from September)

Good afternoon SBA faculty,

As you know, Belleville University will begin offering online distance classes from September, perhaps as one way to showcase the variety of subjects we teach at our school. The President has just asked me for one professor from our department to create and teach a three-month online course.

Advertising for these classes will happen soon, so you would need to submit a syllabus to me by the beginning of March. Why would you volunteer to do this? Well, one benefit of doing this class, besides the extra financial incentive, is that you would not have to participate in some of the tiresome administrative responsibilities the school unfortunately requires from us. In addition, the President and the administration here, who are worried about the success of this new endeavor, would greatly appreciate the extra effort made by these professors.

Let me know if you're interested, then I can fill you in on the details.

Thank you,

James Cameron
Professor, Dean of School of Business Administration
Belleville University

Belleville University

Are you interested in taking a 12-week course taught by highly qualified university professors? Now, you can do so from the comfort of your own home with Belleville University's new online courses.

Classes

Introduction to Modern American Poetry
Professor Honoka Sato

Basics of Law
Professor Jeffrey Hill

Art History
Assistant Professor Mark Cuban

Popular American Music from the 1950s
Lecturer Ted Danson

Business Administration for the Modern World
Professor Yin Lee Chin

Ancient Greek Philosophy
Associate Professor Angela McLeod

Classes start the second week of September.
Those interested please click HERE for more information.
Please double check the computer system requirements needed for each course.
Online registration is on a first-come first-served basis, with a deadline of August 15.

Belleville University Joins World of Online Classes

20 September — It seems every school these days wants to showcase an online learning system. Now, the university found in the downtown of our fair city is no exception.

Last week, Belleville University finally joined the 21st century and started its own online program, presumably to promote itself as a technologically-advanced institution. This initial small-scale endeavor suggests BU is cautiously testing this new frontier, with the possibility of expanding its online learning system in the future.

As the battle intensifies to increase student enrollment numbers to address rising costs, utilizing technology seems imperative for any institution looking to survive.

13. **What is the purpose of this e-mail?**

   (A) To recruit someone for a new project

   (B) To announce a new enrollment policy

   (C) To offer staff more administrative responsibilities

   (D) To inform of changes to work benefits

14. **What is NOT a benefit mentioned by Mr. Cameron?**

   (A) Appreciation from our President

   (B) More money

   (C) Exclusion from annoying work

   (D) Extra vacation time

15. **According to the web page, what must students do?**

   (A) Enroll by the 2nd week of September

   (B) Buy a computer from the school

   (C) Come to the university to register

   (D) Confirm computer system capability

16. **Which faculty member decided to accept Mr. Cameron's offer?**

   (A) Professor Honoka Sato

   (B) Assistant Professor Mark Cuban

   (C) Professor Yin Lee Chin

   (D) Associate Professor Angela McLeod

17. **According to the article, why is creating online learning systems important?**

   (A) It will help the environment.

   (B) It will lessen the need for teachers.

   (C) Schools can decrease administrative work.

   (D) Schools can increase enrollment.

Travel & Hotels 2

Part 5

Incomplete Sentences

Select the best answer to complete the sentence. Then choose the letter (A), (B), (C), or (D).

1. The warm and mineral-rich waters have ------- visitors since ancient times.

   (A) emphasized   (B) relieved   (C) honored   (D) attracted

2. ------- of tourist buses have to attend training seminars to acquire special licenses.

   (A) Operate   (B) Operators   (C) Operations   (D) Operating

3. An ------- version of our city tour will treat you to additional views of Melbourne.

   (A) affordable   (B) essential   (C) extended   (D) immediate

4. The hotel is ------- for its modern interior design and acclaimed restaurants.

   (A) discussed   (B) renowned   (C) limited   (D) accomplished

5. Reservations may be canceled ------- that payment is not made by April 23.

   (A) in order that   (B) such as   (C) in the event   (D) as long as

6. The strikingly ------- gallery has exhibits from many modern artists.

   (A) designs   (B) designed   (C) design   (D) designing

7. This private tour of Ho Chi Minh City ------- you a fascinating insight into the culture and the history.

   (A) is given   (B) gives   (C) to give   (D) giving

8. A professional driver who speaks ------- English will meet you at the airport arrival gate.

   (A) fluent   (B) prompt   (C) practical   (D) demonstrative

Text Completion

Select the best answer to complete the text. Then choose the letter (A), (B), (C), or (D).

Questions 9-12 refer to the following article.

Credit cards are usually the most advantageous way of getting points and miles. Points and miles that can be used to get discounts on airline tickets or everyday ------. ------ on the credit card company, they often offer huge signup
      9.   10.
bonuses of up to 100,000 points or miles.

------ credit cards also offer great ways to get bonus points with your spending
  11.
by creating bonus spending categories where you can earn multiple points at stores and on your phone and Internet bills.

Some credit cards also offer calendar year spending bonuses, such as the USA Premier Rewards Gold, which gives you a 15,000-point bonus when you spend $30,000 or more in a calendar year, essentially giving you a 50% points bonus. ------.
  12.

9. (A) stock   (B) accumulation   (C) manufactures   (D) items

10. (A) Depend   (B) Depends   (C) Depending   (D) Depended

11. (A) Much   (B) Lots   (C) Almost   (D) Many

12. (A) The security risks are great, and people should use credit cards with caution.
    (B) When it comes to credit cards, it really pays to know where the benefits are.
    (C) E-money, though, is becoming more popular than credit cards these days.
    (D) Personalize your credit card by choosing your favorite sports team for the design.

Part 7

Reading Comprehension

Select the best answer for each question and mark the letter (A), (B), (C), or (D).

Questions 13-17 refer to the following web page and e-mails.

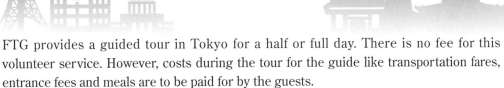

Free Tokyo Guide (FTG)

*** One-day Tours ***

FTG provides a guided tour in Tokyo for a half or full day. There is no fee for this volunteer service. However, costs during the tour for the guide like transportation fares, entrance fees and meals are to be paid for by the guests.

FTG guided tours can begin at the guest's hotel or accommodation, and tours can be taken to any destination within the city limits.

The FTG volunteer guides speak English, with some speaking Spanish, Italian and other languages. Please inquire early about these other language options.

FTG welcomes individuals and groups of up to six people.

To register, please fill out the request form with your contact information and the sites you'd like to visit. You will receive an e-mail directly from a guide when one becomes available.

From: Sana Hashimoto <hashimotosana@geemail.com>
To: Craig McDonald <craigmcdonald@mailman.com>
Date: March 16
Subject: Re: Hotel, etc.

Hello Craig,

It's me again. I'm sorry for all the e-mails today. I've looked for your hotel online but can't seem to find the location. Are you sure you've written the correct hotel name and address on your FTG form? I always ask people to double check their hotel information so that there are no problems on the day of the tour. Please check again and let me know ASAP. The area you're staying in is not far from where I live, so I should be able to walk there to meet you.

Also, you mentioned some of the tourist sites you'd like to visit. I recommend leaving a little sooner than 11:00 A.M., as it will be very busy tomorrow. I can meet you one hour earlier if you'd like.

Let me know what you think.

Sincerely,

Sana

From: Craig McDonald <craigmcdonald@mailman.com>
To: Sana Hashimoto <hashimotosana@geemail.com>
Date: March 16
Subject: Re: Re: Hotel, etc.

Hi Sana,

Let's just meet at an ideal location for both of us. How about in front of West Exit #4 at the train station? Your time suggestion sounds good, but two of my friends have decided not to come on the tour. They'll leave the hotel in the afternoon. It's their last day in Japan and they said they'd like to spend it shopping. That means it'll just be me and my girlfriend, Jane.

Also, let me know your phone number if possible. Here's mine: 999-5188-0222.

See you tomorrow!

Craig

13. On the web page, what is indicated about FTG?

(A) It offers tour guides at different prices.

(B) It gives guests complimentary meals.

(C) It can accommodate groups of any size.

(D) It is flexible with its tours and schedules.

14. What is the purpose of Ms. Hashimoto's e-mail?

(A) To offer suggestions for good tourist sites

(B) To inquire about accommodation information

(C) To confirm the group size

(D) To postpone the meeting time

15. What is indicated about Ms. Hashimoto?

(A) She has recently moved to the city.

(B) She has just started this job.

(C) She is a resident of Tokyo.

(D) She is staying at a nearby hotel.

16. What does Mr. McDonald offer to do?

(A) Meet at a new location

(B) Accompany his friends shopping

(C) Meet at 12:00 noon

(D) Change the tour date

17. In the second e-mail, "spend it" in paragraph 1, line 4, is closest in meaning to

(A) pay money

(B) consume

(C) pass time

(D) reduce something

General

Incomplete Sentences

Select the best answer to complete the sentence. Then choose the letter (A), (B), (C), or (D).

1. In India, new technology will greatly improve their ------- of life.

   (A) qualification   (B) quality   (C) quarter   (D) quantity

2. The board of trustees held a meeting to determine ------- the project can go ahead.

   (A) unless   (B) in order to   (C) how   (D) as if

3. Those companies work closely for the same customer base, but are ------- legal entities.

   (A) precise   (B) separate   (C) certain   (D) primary

4. The government plans to deregulate the system to boost -------.

   (A) to export   (B) exported   (C) exports   (D) exporting

5. Claire was ------- an invaluable asset that she got promoted to a managerial position.

   (A) so   (B) such   (C) only   (D) very

6. The city needs to work on ------- the budget.

   (A) reimbursing   (B) reassigning   (C) recovering   (D) reforming

7. ------- candidates affected by the new election rules should attend the information session.

   (A) Every   (B) Much   (C) Those   (D) Each

8. As the economy gets worse, the public ------- of a tax reduction intensifies.

   (A) anticipation   (B) anticipating   (C) anticipated   (D) anticipate

Part 6

Text Completion

Select the best answer to complete the text. Then choose the letter (A), (B), (C), or (D).

Questions 9-12 refer to the following web page.

Located in one of the most vibrant neighborhoods in New York City is The Rio Hotel. We provide stylish ------ with unmatched service at an affordable price.
9.
The Rio Hotel is the ultimate NYC stay if you want to be in a lively neighborhood ------ by unique shops, nightlife energy, and a thriving local art scene, while
10.
also being steps away from major attractions. Inside of The Rio Hotel ------ our
11.
private event space. It's a cozy space designed to create a state of physical ease and feel like an extension of your living room. ------.
12.

9. (A) goods   (B) amenities   (C) commodities   (D) assets

10. (A) surround   (B) surrounded   (C) is surrounded   (D) surrounding

11. (A) sits   (B) rests   (C) installs   (D) remains

12. (A) Call us today to reserve your live NYC theater tickets.
    (B) For current neighborhood attraction information click here.
    (C) Talk with our staff about including it in your Rio experience.
    (D) To report a problem with your room, call the front desk anytime.

Part 7

Reading Comprehension

Select the best answer for each question and mark the letter (A), (B), (C), or (D).

Questions 13-17 refer to the following web page and e-mails.

---

http://www.cityofburlington.com

City of Burlington Summer Road Closures

Adjust your travel plans accordingly!

Due to ongoing construction and road repair in the city, the following roads will be closed in the month of August. Bus routes are also affected. Sorry for the inconvenience. Please plan your trips wisely.

August 1-3
Lakeshore Road East (from Main Street)

August 4-6
Lakeshore Road West (until Main Street)

August 7-14*
Main Street (downtown, until Highway 5, *subject to change)

August 10-17*
Central Drive (major construction, Brown Street will be used as an alternative, *subject to change)

August 19-22
Dupont Lane (left lane closure, right lane open)

August 23-26
Dupont Lane (right lane closure, left lane open)

August 26-30
Broad Street (major construction, Church Street will be used as an alternative)

Continue to check this website for updates and changes to times and locations.
Contact staff@cityofburlington.com for any questions or concerns.

From: asmith@jwconstruction.com
To: staff@cityofburlington.com
Date: August 2
Subject: Correction

Hello,

My name is Alan Smith. I work for J.W. Construction. We've been hired by the city to do road repairs this summer. Checking with your website, I can see there is a mistake with the information. The construction until the 17th will actually continue for one more day. You should change it to prevent any inconvenience. As far as the Main Street construction: it looks like we'll be finished on the 14th, so that information is correct. This has already been told to staff at City Hall, so I don't know why the website has yet to include this new information.

Thank you,

Alan Smith
Assistant Manager
J.W. Construction

From: staff@cityofburlington.com
To: asmith@jwconstruction.com
Date: August 3
Subject: Re: Correction

Dear Alan,

Thank you for your e-mail. Apparently, your company told a staff member here at City Hall about the changes. However, she left for vacation before telling the person in charge of the website about the updated information. If you check the website now, it should be accurate. In future, feel free to call me directly at 555-9900-4433.

Actually, in February, we had meetings with your company about this summer's construction projects. I don't know if you remember me, but I came up to you after a meeting to mention that our sons are on the same basketball team. Too bad they didn't win much this year.

Anyway, thank you for the e-mail.

Sincerely,

Samantha Brown
Assistant Public Works Officer

13. **What are drivers in Burlington asked to do?**

    (A) Take the bus in August

    (B) Be aware of road changes

    (C) Keep the city roads beautiful

    (D) E-mail construction updates

14. **What road is the first e-mail referring to?**

    (A) Lakeshore Road East

    (B) Lakeshore Road West

    (C) Central Drive

    (D) Dupont Lane

15. **What information is incorrect according to the first e-mail?**

    (A) The street name

    (B) The start date

    (C) The finish date

    (D) The order of construction

16. **Why was the information on the City Hall website incorrect?**

    (A) Nobody told City Hall about the changes.

    (B) The information changed so many times.

    (C) Someone forgot to tell the website operator.

    (D) The website operator forgot to change it.

17. **What do Mr. Smith and Ms. Brown have in common?**

    (A) They live on the same street.

    (B) They like the same sports.

    (C) They have children on the same team.

    (D) They have children who are classmates.

Scene 4

1. Ⓐ Ⓑ Ⓒ Ⓓ   9. Ⓐ Ⓑ Ⓒ Ⓓ
2. Ⓐ Ⓑ Ⓒ Ⓓ   10. Ⓐ Ⓑ Ⓒ Ⓓ
3. Ⓐ Ⓑ Ⓒ Ⓓ   11. Ⓐ Ⓑ Ⓒ Ⓓ
4. Ⓐ Ⓑ Ⓒ Ⓓ   12. Ⓐ Ⓑ Ⓒ Ⓓ
5. Ⓐ Ⓑ Ⓒ Ⓓ   13. Ⓐ Ⓑ Ⓒ Ⓓ
6. Ⓐ Ⓑ Ⓒ Ⓓ   14. Ⓐ Ⓑ Ⓒ Ⓓ
7. Ⓐ Ⓑ Ⓒ Ⓓ   15. Ⓐ Ⓑ Ⓒ Ⓓ
8. Ⓐ Ⓑ Ⓒ Ⓓ   16. Ⓐ Ⓑ Ⓒ Ⓓ
                 17. Ⓐ Ⓑ Ⓒ Ⓓ

STUDENT ID _____

NAME _____

TODAY'S SCORE

Scene 1

1. Ⓐ Ⓑ Ⓒ Ⓓ   9. Ⓐ Ⓑ Ⓒ Ⓓ
2. Ⓐ Ⓑ Ⓒ Ⓓ   10. Ⓐ Ⓑ Ⓒ Ⓓ
3. Ⓐ Ⓑ Ⓒ Ⓓ   11. Ⓐ Ⓑ Ⓒ Ⓓ
4. Ⓐ Ⓑ Ⓒ Ⓓ   12. Ⓐ Ⓑ Ⓒ Ⓓ
5. Ⓐ Ⓑ Ⓒ Ⓓ   13. Ⓐ Ⓑ Ⓒ Ⓓ
6. Ⓐ Ⓑ Ⓒ Ⓓ   14. Ⓐ Ⓑ Ⓒ Ⓓ
7. Ⓐ Ⓑ Ⓒ Ⓓ   15. Ⓐ Ⓑ Ⓒ Ⓓ
8. Ⓐ Ⓑ Ⓒ Ⓓ   16. Ⓐ Ⓑ Ⓒ Ⓓ
                 17. Ⓐ Ⓑ Ⓒ Ⓓ

STUDENT ID _____

NAME _____

TODAY'S SCORE

Scene 5

1. Ⓐ Ⓑ Ⓒ Ⓓ   9. Ⓐ Ⓑ Ⓒ Ⓓ
2. Ⓐ Ⓑ Ⓒ Ⓓ   10. Ⓐ Ⓑ Ⓒ Ⓓ
3. Ⓐ Ⓑ Ⓒ Ⓓ   11. Ⓐ Ⓑ Ⓒ Ⓓ
4. Ⓐ Ⓑ Ⓒ Ⓓ   12. Ⓐ Ⓑ Ⓒ Ⓓ
5. Ⓐ Ⓑ Ⓒ Ⓓ   13. Ⓐ Ⓑ Ⓒ Ⓓ
6. Ⓐ Ⓑ Ⓒ Ⓓ   14. Ⓐ Ⓑ Ⓒ Ⓓ
7. Ⓐ Ⓑ Ⓒ Ⓓ   15. Ⓐ Ⓑ Ⓒ Ⓓ
8. Ⓐ Ⓑ Ⓒ Ⓓ   16. Ⓐ Ⓑ Ⓒ Ⓓ
                 17. Ⓐ Ⓑ Ⓒ Ⓓ

STUDENT ID _____

NAME _____

TODAY'S SCORE

Scene 2

1. Ⓐ Ⓑ Ⓒ Ⓓ   9. Ⓐ Ⓑ Ⓒ Ⓓ
2. Ⓐ Ⓑ Ⓒ Ⓓ   10. Ⓐ Ⓑ Ⓒ Ⓓ
3. Ⓐ Ⓑ Ⓒ Ⓓ   11. Ⓐ Ⓑ Ⓒ Ⓓ
4. Ⓐ Ⓑ Ⓒ Ⓓ   12. Ⓐ Ⓑ Ⓒ Ⓓ
5. Ⓐ Ⓑ Ⓒ Ⓓ   13. Ⓐ Ⓑ Ⓒ Ⓓ
6. Ⓐ Ⓑ Ⓒ Ⓓ   14. Ⓐ Ⓑ Ⓒ Ⓓ
7. Ⓐ Ⓑ Ⓒ Ⓓ   15. Ⓐ Ⓑ Ⓒ Ⓓ
8. Ⓐ Ⓑ Ⓒ Ⓓ   16. Ⓐ Ⓑ Ⓒ Ⓓ
                 17. Ⓐ Ⓑ Ⓒ Ⓓ

STUDENT ID _____

NAME _____

TODAY'S SCORE

Scene 6

1. Ⓐ Ⓑ Ⓒ Ⓓ   9. Ⓐ Ⓑ Ⓒ Ⓓ
2. Ⓐ Ⓑ Ⓒ Ⓓ   10. Ⓐ Ⓑ Ⓒ Ⓓ
3. Ⓐ Ⓑ Ⓒ Ⓓ   11. Ⓐ Ⓑ Ⓒ Ⓓ
4. Ⓐ Ⓑ Ⓒ Ⓓ   12. Ⓐ Ⓑ Ⓒ Ⓓ
5. Ⓐ Ⓑ Ⓒ Ⓓ   13. Ⓐ Ⓑ Ⓒ Ⓓ
6. Ⓐ Ⓑ Ⓒ Ⓓ   14. Ⓐ Ⓑ Ⓒ Ⓓ
7. Ⓐ Ⓑ Ⓒ Ⓓ   15. Ⓐ Ⓑ Ⓒ Ⓓ
8. Ⓐ Ⓑ Ⓒ Ⓓ   16. Ⓐ Ⓑ Ⓒ Ⓓ
                 17. Ⓐ Ⓑ Ⓒ Ⓓ

STUDENT ID _____

NAME _____

TODAY'S SCORE

Scene 3

1. Ⓐ Ⓑ Ⓒ Ⓓ   9. Ⓐ Ⓑ Ⓒ Ⓓ
2. Ⓐ Ⓑ Ⓒ Ⓓ   10. Ⓐ Ⓑ Ⓒ Ⓓ
3. Ⓐ Ⓑ Ⓒ Ⓓ   11. Ⓐ Ⓑ Ⓒ Ⓓ
4. Ⓐ Ⓑ Ⓒ Ⓓ   12. Ⓐ Ⓑ Ⓒ Ⓓ
5. Ⓐ Ⓑ Ⓒ Ⓓ   13. Ⓐ Ⓑ Ⓒ Ⓓ
6. Ⓐ Ⓑ Ⓒ Ⓓ   14. Ⓐ Ⓑ Ⓒ Ⓓ
7. Ⓐ Ⓑ Ⓒ Ⓓ   15. Ⓐ Ⓑ Ⓒ Ⓓ
8. Ⓐ Ⓑ Ⓒ Ⓓ   16. Ⓐ Ⓑ Ⓒ Ⓓ
                 17. Ⓐ Ⓑ Ⓒ Ⓓ

STUDENT ID _____

NAME _____

TODAY'S SCORE

Scene 10

1. Ⓐ Ⓑ Ⓒ Ⓓ
2. Ⓐ Ⓑ Ⓒ Ⓓ
3. Ⓐ Ⓑ Ⓒ Ⓓ
4. Ⓐ Ⓑ Ⓒ Ⓓ
5. Ⓐ Ⓑ Ⓒ Ⓓ
6. Ⓐ Ⓑ Ⓒ Ⓓ
7. Ⓐ Ⓑ Ⓒ Ⓓ
8. Ⓐ Ⓑ Ⓒ Ⓓ

9. Ⓐ Ⓑ Ⓒ Ⓓ
10. Ⓐ Ⓑ Ⓒ Ⓓ
11. Ⓐ Ⓑ Ⓒ Ⓓ
12. Ⓐ Ⓑ Ⓒ Ⓓ
13. Ⓐ Ⓑ Ⓒ Ⓓ
14. Ⓐ Ⓑ Ⓒ Ⓓ
15. Ⓐ Ⓑ Ⓒ Ⓓ
16. Ⓐ Ⓑ Ⓒ Ⓓ
17. Ⓐ Ⓑ Ⓒ Ⓓ

STUDENT ID

NAME

TODAY'S SCORE

Scene 7

DATE   /   /

1. Ⓐ Ⓑ Ⓒ Ⓓ
2. Ⓐ Ⓑ Ⓒ Ⓓ
3. Ⓐ Ⓑ Ⓒ Ⓓ
4. Ⓐ Ⓑ Ⓒ Ⓓ
5. Ⓐ Ⓑ Ⓒ Ⓓ
6. Ⓐ Ⓑ Ⓒ Ⓓ
7. Ⓐ Ⓑ Ⓒ Ⓓ
8. Ⓐ Ⓑ Ⓒ Ⓓ

9. Ⓐ Ⓑ Ⓒ Ⓓ
10. Ⓐ Ⓑ Ⓒ Ⓓ
11. Ⓐ Ⓑ Ⓒ Ⓓ
12. Ⓐ Ⓑ Ⓒ Ⓓ
13. Ⓐ Ⓑ Ⓒ Ⓓ
14. Ⓐ Ⓑ Ⓒ Ⓓ
15. Ⓐ Ⓑ Ⓒ Ⓓ
16. Ⓐ Ⓑ Ⓒ Ⓓ
17. Ⓐ Ⓑ Ⓒ Ⓓ

STUDENT ID

NAME

TODAY'S SCORE

Scene 11

DATE   /   /

1. Ⓐ Ⓑ Ⓒ Ⓓ
2. Ⓐ Ⓑ Ⓒ Ⓓ
3. Ⓐ Ⓑ Ⓒ Ⓓ
4. Ⓐ Ⓑ Ⓒ Ⓓ
5. Ⓐ Ⓑ Ⓒ Ⓓ
6. Ⓐ Ⓑ Ⓒ Ⓓ
7. Ⓐ Ⓑ Ⓒ Ⓓ
8. Ⓐ Ⓑ Ⓒ Ⓓ

9. Ⓐ Ⓑ Ⓒ Ⓓ
10. Ⓐ Ⓑ Ⓒ Ⓓ
11. Ⓐ Ⓑ Ⓒ Ⓓ
12. Ⓐ Ⓑ Ⓒ Ⓓ
13. Ⓐ Ⓑ Ⓒ Ⓓ
14. Ⓐ Ⓑ Ⓒ Ⓓ
15. Ⓐ Ⓑ Ⓒ Ⓓ
16. Ⓐ Ⓑ Ⓒ Ⓓ
17. Ⓐ Ⓑ Ⓒ Ⓓ

STUDENT ID

NAME

TODAY'S SCORE

Scene 8

DATE   /   /

1. Ⓐ Ⓑ Ⓒ Ⓓ
2. Ⓐ Ⓑ Ⓒ Ⓓ
3. Ⓐ Ⓑ Ⓒ Ⓓ
4. Ⓐ Ⓑ Ⓒ Ⓓ
5. Ⓐ Ⓑ Ⓒ Ⓓ
6. Ⓐ Ⓑ Ⓒ Ⓓ
7. Ⓐ Ⓑ Ⓒ Ⓓ
8. Ⓐ Ⓑ Ⓒ Ⓓ
9. Ⓐ Ⓑ Ⓒ Ⓓ

10. Ⓐ Ⓑ Ⓒ Ⓓ
11. Ⓐ Ⓑ Ⓒ Ⓓ
12. Ⓐ Ⓑ Ⓒ Ⓓ
13. Ⓐ Ⓑ Ⓒ Ⓓ
14. Ⓐ Ⓑ Ⓒ Ⓓ
15. Ⓐ Ⓑ Ⓒ Ⓓ
16. Ⓐ Ⓑ Ⓒ Ⓓ
17. Ⓐ Ⓑ Ⓒ Ⓓ
18. Ⓐ Ⓑ Ⓒ Ⓓ

STUDENT ID

NAME

TODAY'S SCORE

Scene 12

DATE   /   /

1. Ⓐ Ⓑ Ⓒ Ⓓ
2. Ⓐ Ⓑ Ⓒ Ⓓ
3. Ⓐ Ⓑ Ⓒ Ⓓ
4. Ⓐ Ⓑ Ⓒ Ⓓ
5. Ⓐ Ⓑ Ⓒ Ⓓ
6. Ⓐ Ⓑ Ⓒ Ⓓ
7. Ⓐ Ⓑ Ⓒ Ⓓ
8. Ⓐ Ⓑ Ⓒ Ⓓ

9. Ⓐ Ⓑ Ⓒ Ⓓ
10. Ⓐ Ⓑ Ⓒ Ⓓ
11. Ⓐ Ⓑ Ⓒ Ⓓ
12. Ⓐ Ⓑ Ⓒ Ⓓ
13. Ⓐ Ⓑ Ⓒ Ⓓ
14. Ⓐ Ⓑ Ⓒ Ⓓ
15. Ⓐ Ⓑ Ⓒ Ⓓ
16. Ⓐ Ⓑ Ⓒ Ⓓ
17. Ⓐ Ⓑ Ⓒ Ⓓ

STUDENT ID

NAME

TODAY'S SCORE

Scene 9

DATE   /   /

1. Ⓐ Ⓑ Ⓒ Ⓓ
2. Ⓐ Ⓑ Ⓒ Ⓓ
3. Ⓐ Ⓑ Ⓒ Ⓓ
4. Ⓐ Ⓑ Ⓒ Ⓓ
5. Ⓐ Ⓑ Ⓒ Ⓓ
6. Ⓐ Ⓑ Ⓒ Ⓓ
7. Ⓐ Ⓑ Ⓒ Ⓓ
8. Ⓐ Ⓑ Ⓒ Ⓓ

9. Ⓐ Ⓑ Ⓒ Ⓓ
10. Ⓐ Ⓑ Ⓒ Ⓓ
11. Ⓐ Ⓑ Ⓒ Ⓓ
12. Ⓐ Ⓑ Ⓒ Ⓓ
13. Ⓐ Ⓑ Ⓒ Ⓓ
14. Ⓐ Ⓑ Ⓒ Ⓓ
15. Ⓐ Ⓑ Ⓒ Ⓓ
16. Ⓐ Ⓑ Ⓒ Ⓓ

STUDENT ID

NAME

TODAY'S SCORE

Scene 13

DATE ___ / ___ / ___

1. Ⓐ Ⓑ Ⓒ Ⓓ
2. Ⓐ Ⓑ Ⓒ Ⓓ
3. Ⓐ Ⓑ Ⓒ Ⓓ
4. Ⓐ Ⓑ Ⓒ Ⓓ
5. Ⓐ Ⓑ Ⓒ Ⓓ
6. Ⓐ Ⓑ Ⓒ Ⓓ
7. Ⓐ Ⓑ Ⓒ Ⓓ
8. Ⓐ Ⓑ Ⓒ Ⓓ

9. Ⓐ Ⓑ Ⓒ Ⓓ
10. Ⓐ Ⓑ Ⓒ Ⓓ
11. Ⓐ Ⓑ Ⓒ Ⓓ
12. Ⓐ Ⓑ Ⓒ Ⓓ
13. Ⓐ Ⓑ Ⓒ Ⓓ
14. Ⓐ Ⓑ Ⓒ Ⓓ
15. Ⓐ Ⓑ Ⓒ Ⓓ
16. Ⓐ Ⓑ Ⓒ Ⓓ
17. Ⓐ Ⓑ Ⓒ Ⓓ

STUDENT ID _____

NAME _____

TODAY'S SCORE

Scene 14

DATE ___ / ___ / ___

1. Ⓐ Ⓑ Ⓒ Ⓓ
2. Ⓐ Ⓑ Ⓒ Ⓓ
3. Ⓐ Ⓑ Ⓒ Ⓓ
4. Ⓐ Ⓑ Ⓒ Ⓓ
5. Ⓐ Ⓑ Ⓒ Ⓓ
6. Ⓐ Ⓑ Ⓒ Ⓓ
7. Ⓐ Ⓑ Ⓒ Ⓓ
8. Ⓐ Ⓑ Ⓒ Ⓓ

9. Ⓐ Ⓑ Ⓒ Ⓓ
10. Ⓐ Ⓑ Ⓒ Ⓓ
11. Ⓐ Ⓑ Ⓒ Ⓓ
12. Ⓐ Ⓑ Ⓒ Ⓓ
13. Ⓐ Ⓑ Ⓒ Ⓓ
14. Ⓐ Ⓑ Ⓒ Ⓓ
15. Ⓐ Ⓑ Ⓒ Ⓓ
16. Ⓐ Ⓑ Ⓒ Ⓓ
17. Ⓐ Ⓑ Ⓒ Ⓓ

STUDENT ID _____

NAME _____

TODAY'S SCORE

Scene 15

DATE ___ / ___ / ___

1. Ⓐ Ⓑ Ⓒ Ⓓ
2. Ⓐ Ⓑ Ⓒ Ⓓ
3. Ⓐ Ⓑ Ⓒ Ⓓ
4. Ⓐ Ⓑ Ⓒ Ⓓ
5. Ⓐ Ⓑ Ⓒ Ⓓ
6. Ⓐ Ⓑ Ⓒ Ⓓ
7. Ⓐ Ⓑ Ⓒ Ⓓ
8. Ⓐ Ⓑ Ⓒ Ⓓ

9. Ⓐ Ⓑ Ⓒ Ⓓ
10. Ⓐ Ⓑ Ⓒ Ⓓ
11. Ⓐ Ⓑ Ⓒ Ⓓ
12. Ⓐ Ⓑ Ⓒ Ⓓ
13. Ⓐ Ⓑ Ⓒ Ⓓ
14. Ⓐ Ⓑ Ⓒ Ⓓ
15. Ⓐ Ⓑ Ⓒ Ⓓ
16. Ⓐ Ⓑ Ⓒ Ⓓ
17. Ⓐ Ⓑ Ⓒ Ⓓ

STUDENT ID _____

NAME _____

TODAY'S SCORE

PROFILE／著者略歴

Matthew Wilson（マシュー・ウィルソン）
宮城大学基盤教育群教授。
カナダ・トロント出身。カナダ、韓国、日本で長年、英語教育に携わる。仙台市教育委員会教育アドバイザーを経て2009年より宮城大学事業構想学部准教授、2016年より同教授、2017年より現職。研究分野は日本における英語教育と学生の動機づけ。米国のシェナンドア大学大学院卒業。同校より修士号取得（TESOL）。

鶴岡 公幸（つるおか ともゆき）
神田外語大学外国語学部教授。
神奈川県横浜市出身。キッコーマン（株）、（財）国際ビジネスコミュニケーション協会、KPMGあずさ監査法人、宮城大学食産業学部を経て、2014年より現職。1998年インディアナ大学経営大学院卒業。同校より経営学修士（MBA）取得。専門はマーケティング、ビジネス英語。TOEIC®関連書籍を含め著書、テキスト多数。

佐藤 千春（さとう ちはる）
株式会社and ENGLISH代表取締役。
山形県出身。岩手大学人文社会科学部卒業。山形県公立中学校英語教諭として14年間勤務。社会教育主事補資格取得。退職後、都内TOEIC®専門校講師兼マネージャーとしての勤務を経て、英語スクール『株式会社and ENGLISH』を起業。編集協力としてTOEIC®単語集の出版に携わる。

QUICK EXERCISES FOR THE TOEIC® L&R TEST 600 Reading
切り取り提出式 スコア別 TOEIC® L&R徹底対策ドリル600 リーディング編

2021年4月5日　初版第1刷発行

著　　者　Matthew Wilson／鶴岡公幸／佐藤千春

発 行 者　森　信久
発 行 所　**株式会社　松柏社**
　　　　　〒102-0072　東京都千代田区飯田橋1-6-1
　　　　　TEL　03（3230）4813（代表）
　　　　　FAX　03（3230）4857
　　　　　http://www.shohakusha.com
　　　　　e-mail: info@shohakusha.com

装　　幀　小島トシノブ（NONdesign）
本文レイアウト　　赤木健太郎（有限会社ケークルーデザインワークス）
組版・印刷・製本　シナノ書籍印刷株式会社
ISBN978-4-88198-766-7
略号＝766

Copyright © 2021 by Matthew Wilson, Tomoyuki Tsuruoka and Chiharu Sato